BROTHERS † WOMACK

PUBLISHING LLC

DEDICATIONS

To my Dad, Todd Andre Womack:
Thank you for always being there for me and inspiring me to do the best that I can.
I love you,
Ande

To my Jamaican Grandmother, Hazel Gordon,
and my Great Aunt, Sybil Blount:
Thank you for introducing me to Anancy, and the Art of Storytelling.
Love you and miss you,
Shani

ACKNOWLEDGEMENTS

Inspired by the Anansi Stories that originated in West Africa. These stories were often one of the only things those kidnapped from Africa could carry with them across the ocean. These stories were handed down from one generation to the next; a source of connectivity, creativity and strength, that still endures. We decided to create a new story to add to the collection. Anancy stories are great for reading, but they are made to be told. I encourage readers to memorize this story and tell it over and over again, to a friend, a classmate, a neighbor and or family member.

(Don't forget to try your best Jamaican accent!)

ONCE UPON A TIME,

when the world was new and long before the sea was salty, there lived a little spider named Anancy. If you know anything about Anancy, you would know that he was no ordinary, common spider. He had special powers to change himself into a man and back into a spider again. Anancy is the original spider-man!

ANANCY

It was a beautiful Saturday morning and Anancy woke up early.
He washed his face, got dressed, and cleaned his house.
He was preparing for a dinner party.
Anancy had invited some new friends over for Sunday dinner and he wanted to make a good impression.
Everything had to be perfect.
By noon, he left home to go to the market to buy fresh spices and seasonings for his special meal. He bought thyme and garlic, curry powder and fresh ground black pepper. He found everything he needed except for salt. All of the market vendors said they were out of this precious ingredient.

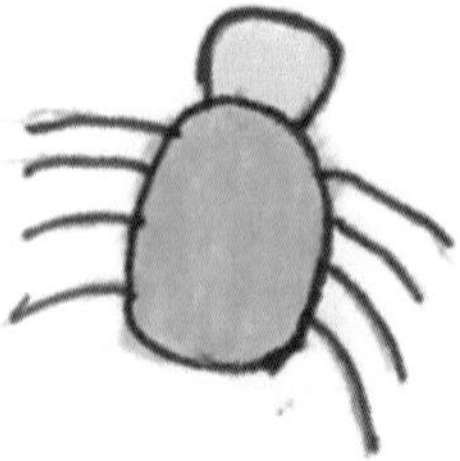

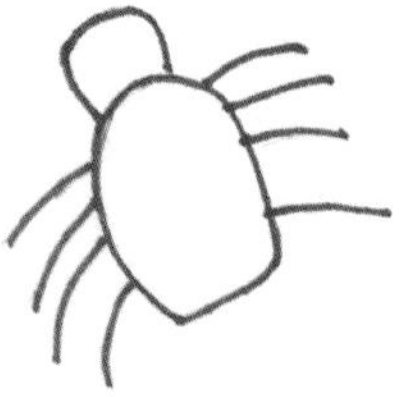

This was terrible news! Anancy could not make his famous curry chicken without salt. Anancy decided to go directly to the salt mine in search of this savory seasoning. When he got there, the mine was closed and the entrance was boarded up. As Anancy looked around, wondering what to do next, an old man came walking by. He said, "they had to close the mine, because there was no more salt left inside". All that was left were gray rocks... no salt. Anancy was frustrated and sad. Without salt, his meal would be too bland. He would certainly not impress his new friends.

SALT. MINE
CLOSED

As he made his way home, he got an idea. Anancy thought, "What if I could find more salt? Maybe there is another salt mine somewhere? I could bring the salt back here to my village. I could sell it to everyone in the market. Then, I would really impress my new friends and become a hero. I could also become very rich." Anancy laughed to himself. With that, he called his new friends and canceled the dinner party. He sat at his kitchen table and wrote out his plans. By the next morning, he had convinced two of his oldest friends, Tiger and Pig, to go with him on a search for salt.

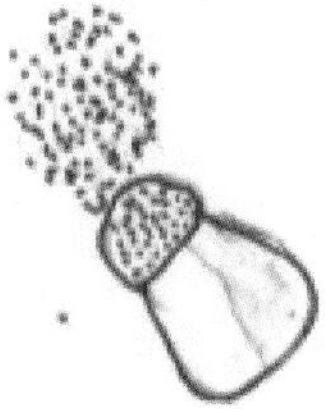

Anancy promised to share the money he hoped to make from the salt with Tiger. Tiger, in return let him use his boat. Anancy promised Pig a month of savory, salty dishes when they returned home, if Pig would let Anancy use his raft. Pig agreed. So, they set off to cross the sea to find another island with a salt cave. The weather was beautiful, not a cloud in the sky.

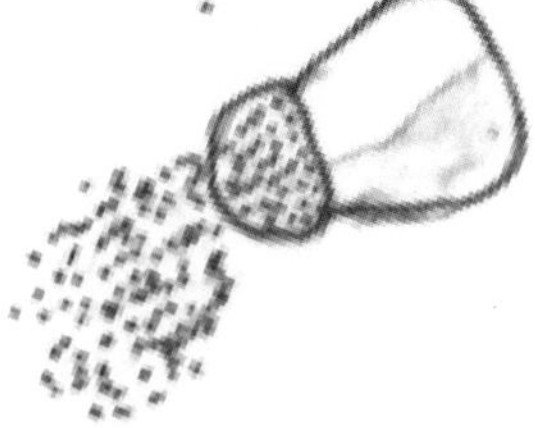

Anancy navigated while Tiger and Pig took turns rowing. It took them all day to get to the next island. When they made it across the sea, they began to look for a cave. Pig was perfect for this job as he had a nose that could sniff out the scent of salt. In no time at all, Pig led them to a cave. “I think I’ve found it!” he said.

Tiger went in and licked one of the walls just to confirm it.

“It’s salt!” he said. “The walls are made of salt!”

Anancy jumped for joy and shouted, “I’m going to be rich! I mean, we are going to be rich!”

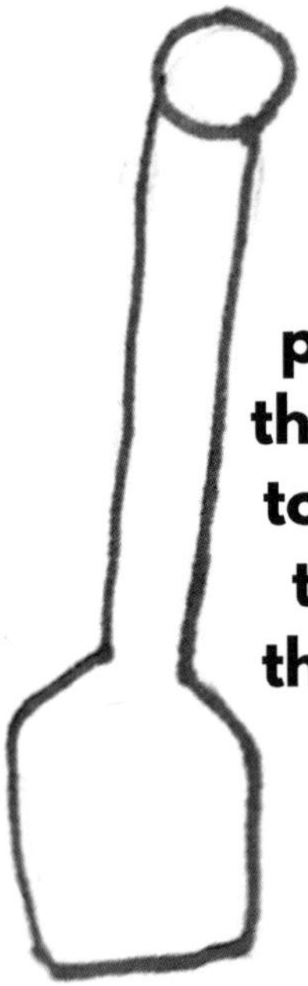

Anancy grabbed his tools; he had brought three chisels, two hammers, one saw, two shovels, and a large tarp. They worked for the next few days collecting the rock salt. They all hammered and chiseled at the walls, then Tiger cut the salt into blocks from the walls in the cave. Anancy would place the blocks on top of the tarp, Pig would haul the tarp full of salt to the raft. The raft was attached to the back of the boat, down near the beach. Once the raft and the boat were full with blocks of salt, they used their shovels to scoop up all the crumbled and crushed pieces of salt; they shoveled it into mounds. They took as much as they could carry. Anancy didn't want to leave anything behind.

There was barely enough room for all three of them to fit into the boat, but they somehow managed to squeeze in. Pig and Tiger took turns rowing the boat while Anancy navigated and watched the sky. About half way through the journey he saw clouds in the distance and he knew: this was not good. He began to worry, but he didn't tell Pig or Tiger. He only said to them, "row faster! Row faster!" Pig and Tiger were tired after several days of working in the mines with little rest, they both began to complain. "My poor back is aching," said Pig.

"My arms are sore," said Tiger.

Anancy said again, "row faster! Row faster!"

But Pig and Tiger refused to row any farther and demanded, "Anancy you take over, since you have 8 arms!" Anancy did not want to row the boat, but he saw the dark clouds ahead and felt the wind was picking up speed. Anancy knew they had to get home quickly. He grabbed the oars from Pig and said "hurry, we must row faster! Row faster!"

He began to row wildly.

Anancy was nervous about the approaching storm.
He knew what it would do to his precious salt.
He couldn't quite coordinate his arms to work together. Pig laughed at him and said "row faster, row faster!" "Yeah...this trip was your idea!" said Tiger. While they were laughing, it began to sprinkle.

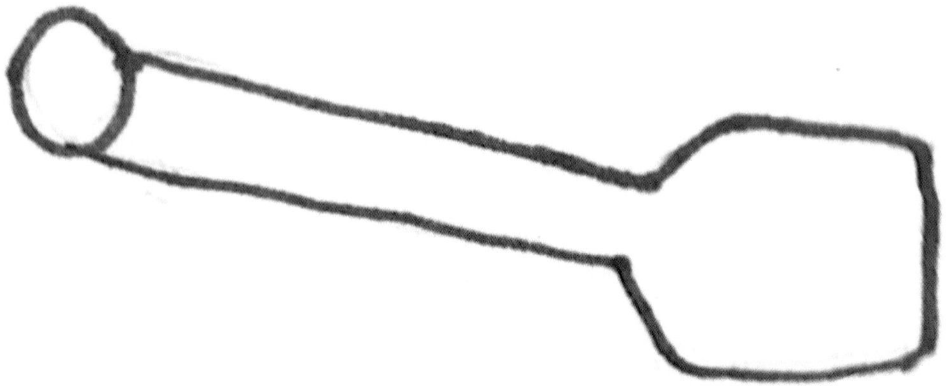

Pig and Tiger stopped laughing and urged Anancy to, “row faster! Row faster!” Anancy tried his best to pick up the pace; they could see the shore in the distance, as a steady rain started. The wind blew harder and harder, and the sky turned black.

The waves started to whip up against the sides of the boat. Pig stuck his hooves into the water and began to paddle as fast as he could.

Tiger cried out “row faster, row faster!”

And they all rowed as fast as they could.

By now, rain was pouring from the sky. The salt was damp. Pig tried to help by laying on top of the salt, covering it with his body. But the rain continued to pour down on the precious salt and it began to melt. "Oh my" cried Anancy, "my salt... my savory salt!" The sea turned violently, the waves splashed up onto the raft and into the boat. Enormous raindrops splashed down on the salt! It began to drain off the sides of the raft and into the sea. Before they could get to the shore the entire boat tipped and then flipped over.

Anancy, Pig and Tiger realized they had to leave everything behind and swim for their lives! They all made it safely to shore, but not even one grain of salt survived the journey.
All that hard work for nothing!
That is how salt got into the sea.
It is Anancy who made the sea salty!
Anancy Mek it...
Jack Mandora, me nah choose none!

THE END

“Jack Mandora, me nah choose none”

**Every Jamaican Anancy story ends with this phrase.
It simply means: Just in case this story is not true,
I am not responsible. The storyteller
uses this disclaimer,
in hopes that Jack Mandora,
(the keeper of Heavens’ gates)
will not deny them entrance,
because of telling lies.**

COLORING PAGES

ANANCY

Printed in Great Britain
by Amazon

34049772R00018